The Pain Is Real, But The Promise Is Eternal: What To Do When God's Will Hurts

By: Whitney J. Hogans

Published May 2017 by *She Heals Publishing*
www.shehealspublishing.com

She Heals Publishing

Dedication

This book is in memory of my late husband, Stephen Anthony Hogans. Thank you for your love, support, and example. No matter where life takes me, I'll never forget you. I love you, forever.

This book is dedicated to my precious sons. Quincy & Kevin. Words cannot express how much I love you both.

Thank You

I would first like to thank my Lord and Savior, Jesus Christ, I am nothing apart from Him. I would also like to thank Quincy & Kevin, my precious sons. I thank God that out of all the women in the world, He chose me to be the mother of these two amazing young boys. I want to thank my parents, Floyd Lyles & Linda Allen for their love and support. Mom, I never thought that God would allow you to leave this earth so early, but I trust His plan. I love you and I miss you.

Thanks to my father, Floyd Lyles for being a huge help to the boys and I the last few years particularly. I want to thank all my siblings Lea, Sherae, Dave, Michael, Georgia, and Jordan, I love you all. I want to thank all my family for being my rock. I want to especially thank my aunts Barbara Ambush & Beverly Hall for being my role models. You two have blessed me beyond what I could say. I want to thank my two cousins who are my best friends, Lashierya Parker & Keynora Greenwood, cousins by blood, sisters by heart. Thank you guys for the prayers and encouragement during the creation of this book. I want to thank my in laws for all of their love and support. I especially want to thank my mother-in-law, Barbara Hayward. You are my Naomi and I am your Ruth. Thank you for loving me and walking me through the journey of being a young widow and mother. I could not do it without you. I also want to thank my church family, Messiah Community Church for all of their prayers and support. Thank you to Clifton Cothorne for the creation of the book cover, it is amazing! Special thanks also goes to my amazing Editors Melvin Worthington III, & Samantha McCoy. I am truly thankful for you guys partnering with me!

Last but never least, I want to thank my late husband Stephen. Thank you for believing in me before I ever believed in myself. I am forever grateful to you. I am grateful for all the people who love me, have supported me in any way, prayed for me, etc. If I left anyone out, please charge it to my head and not my heart. I am truly thankful!

Table of Contents

I.   Introduction
II. Part 1: The Pain
III. Part 2: The Promise
IV. Part 3: The Process
V.   Part 4: The Purpose
VI. Part 5: Final Thoughts

Introduction

Disclaimer: If you are looking for a book to read that is about a perfect Christian woman who trusts God through everything, never once questions God and is okay with everything He allows, then this is not the book for you. If you are, however, looking for an honest picture of what trusting God and submitting to God truly entails: the good times, the bad times, the process, then this is the book for you! This book is not about me showing you my best self. The purpose of this book is for you to see just how much of a hot mess I am and just how loving, kind, faithful, merciful and wonderful the God I serve is. Interested? Keep reading ☺

Prayer

Lord,

This is your daughter, Whitney. I am coming to you because I am afraid. I know you do not give us the spirit of fear but I am being honest God…I am afraid. I am afraid to be this open. I am afraid that maybe I shared too much or not enough. Will the book bless people? Are you pleased with me? Are you pleased with this book? Lord, I have so many thoughts and feelings running through my mind, but there is one thing I do know; this book is Your will. Since I know it is Your will, I know You are pleased. I must cast out those thoughts that say otherwise.

Lord, please lead whomever is intended to read this book to it. Please open their mind and heart. Most of all, God, heal them. They are hurting and they need you, whether they know it or not. Lord, do what only you can do. May you get the glory out of everything that I do. Thank you for choosing me for this journey, even the moments that hurt. I give my all to you. I trust you and I praise you. Your will be done.

Love,
Whitney

Pain

*For I am about to fall, and my **pain** is ever with me.*
Psalm 38:17

Oftentimes as Christians we say things but we don't really mean them. We may say them out of habit or routine but we do not always feel it. One of the things that we say a lot is "God's will be done." We say that and it sounds great. Oftentimes when we say that what we actually mean is "Lord, I want Your will, but I want it according to my comfort. Really, I want you to be okay with my will." We want God's will because we believe God's will is always good. The harsh truth is that sometimes God's will allow things that can hurt us, even devastate us. Sometimes, God's will causes us pain. Sometimes things can happen that make us question our faith in God. Anger and confusion cause us to drift from God. This book is not going to be pretty, but it is honest. I am not an expert, I am just a woman who pressed through a really hard time (I'll explain later) and felt every ounce of pain. The pain is REAL, but the PROMISE is eternal. Here is my take on what to do when God's will hurts.

Pain is inevitable. Since we live in a sinful world, we can anticipate pain from time to time. Clearly pain is a part of life but for some reason, many of us Christians think that we are immune to pain. We think that once we say yes to God that we are free from life's trials. Surely God would not continue to allow pain to occur *after* you gave your life to Him, right?

I remember having testimony service at church as a kid. I loved hearing people testify. First they would share the problem and then what God did. The church would erupt in praise! While the testimonies were powerful, I couldn't help but wonder – what happened in between the time the problems occurred and when God stepped in? Did the person have complete security in God and never doubted? What does trust in God really feel like?

I thought I knew pain pretty well. Over the years, I experienced hard times, heartbreak and even gave birth to two sons (childbirth is no joke!) I had many tests in trusting God throughout my life, and while I had periods of doubt and unbelief, I persevered and my faith remained. Then, 2012 came and God allowed me to go through an unspeakable pain – one of the deepest heartbreaks of my life. After this pain occurred, I was not sure how I would ever recover.

I started 2012 with crazy faith! I was 25, a wife and mother of two, and excitedly passionate about God. At the time, my family was in serious need of miracles. My husband Steve, who was 30, was quite ill at the beginning of that year and needed a double lung transplant for the second time. My youngest son, Kevin, was two and was not speaking, making eye contact, or interacting properly with others. We were also going through hard times financially. However, my faith was so strong that I was not worried. The worse things got, the more I praised God. I just knew that He would bring the healing and providence that we needed. I thought, "It doesn't matter how it looks, God will turn it around!"

My husband came into my life shortly after I re-dedicated my life to Christ. He was the most incredible man I'd ever met. He was a man of faith, totally submitted to God; determined to live the life God had for Him. He inspired me to be better. Surely, God was not going to take him. God saw that I was only 25 and my sons were only 5 and 2, too young to lose such a great man. God had given Steve new lungs before, of course he would do it again!

The funny thing about God's will is that it will happen whether you are in agreement with it or not. On July 5, 2012, My husband Steve died just twenty days shy of his 31st birthday. Not only did I lose my husband, my absolute soulmate and best friend, but I also had a few new challenges. My son Kevin was diagnosed with Autism the same year.

I was now a 25-year-old widow, single mom to two boys, working full time as a Special Education Paraeducator (making $23,000 a year) and was in school full time to become a Special Education Teacher. This was my breaking point. Many nights, I cried out "God how could you? Why? Why him? Why me?" I was mad at God! He destroyed my life! He took so much from me at once. Not only did I become a widow, I was also a single working mom and a parent of a child with a disability. Why would God allow so much pain?

Looking back, I realize that I did not have the proper perspective. I naively thought that following God meant a pain-free life; I thought my days of struggle were over forever. I never took the time to read about what God says about pain and hard times. I was not prepared to be disappointed by what He allowed. I did not know how to share my feelings of hurt, anger and frustration with Him – how dare I question His sovereignty?

Truth be told, will face pain as Christians. We will also experience tragedy. God never promised us a pain free journey, but He does promise us that he will be with us along the way. There is a process involved, a process that we as Christians don't always feel comfortable talking about. Before we get to the process we must establish some truths. Again I say, if you are looking for a feel good book, stop reading now. If you are ready for some raw truth, then continue ☺

Truth #1: God Allows Pain

We give the enemy too much credit. Every time something bad happens, we blame the enemy. What we forget is that God is omnipotent; he is all powerful. Nothing happens without his permission. Even the enemy has to submit to the authority of God. Don't take my word for it, let's go to the word of God. If you go to the book of Job, you will see clearly what I mean. In the first chapter of Job, the bible describes Job as "blameless & upright". Job was a great man! He followed God, did the right thing and lived an honorable life. Let's take a look at what happens in Job 1:6-8.

[6] *Now there was a day when the sons of God came to present themselves before the Lord, and Satan[a] also came among them.* [7] *The Lord said to Satan, "From where have you come?" Satan answered the Lord and said, "From going to and fro on the earth, and from walking up and down on it."* [8] *And the Lord said to Satan, "Have you considered my servant Job, that there is none like him on the earth, a blameless and upright man, who fears God and turns away from evil?" (ESV)*

What just happened here? God is talking to Satan? God offered Job to be tested by the enemy? Yes, yes He did! Want to know why? It is because God knew His child! He knew that Job could endure the tests even before they became reality. He knew who Job was! Would you believe me if I told you that God has had a conversation about you? Satan needed permission from God before he could ever touch you. Your pain did not catch God by surprise, He allowed it.

I know you are thinking, "Why would God allow pain?" I asked myself the same question. Make no mistake – the enemy seeks to destroy us, but he can only do what God allows. As much as we want to think that God is not involved when pain exists, He never leaves us or forsakes us. He is omnipresent, which means He is there before, during and after our pain. You may be asking, "What is the benefit of a relationship with God if He does not shield us from pain?"

This may be a harsh truth for some but it is true…God allows pain. Before we get all bent out of shape let's read the rest of this paragraph.
The encounter continues between God and Satan in verses 9-12:

^{9} "Does Job fear God for nothing?" Satan replied. ^{10} "Have you not put a hedge around him and his household and everything he has? You have blessed the work of his hands, so that his flocks and herds are spread throughout the land. ^{11} But now stretch out your hand and strike everything he has, and he will surely curse you to your face."
^{12} The Lord said to Satan, "Very well, then, everything he has is in your power, but on the man himself do not lay a finger."
Then Satan went out from the presence of the Lord."

Truth #2: Your Pain Has Limitations

God allows us to go through things at times but there are limitations. God may allow the enemy to test us but the enemy does not have full authority to do whatever he wants; he only can do what God allows. God told Satan that he could attack Job but that he could not touch Job. God has parameters around your pain. I always hear the saying, "God doesn't give you more than you can bear." I personally disagree. I think sometimes God does give us more than we can bear as a reminder to lean on him. He puts pressure on us to increase our dependence on Him. We don't need to handle it all in our own strength.

Sometimes we weigh ourselves down with burdens and battles we weren't meant to carry. We pray, but we do not believe that God will intervene. So, we finish our prayers and then try to solve the problems on our own, leading to exhaustion and disappointment. God wants us to lean on him. He wants our total trust.

Truth #3: God Never Allows You To Be In Pain Alone

When God allows us to experience pain, He always provides support. The enemy wants us to feel isolated in our pain and feel like we are the only ones suffering. However, even when you are physically alone, God has assigned people to pray for you. God provides strength and comfort even when you do not realize it. After a night of depression and suicidal thoughts, somehow you manage to make it through to the next day. Your endurance is possible because of someone's prayers.

God aligned me with an amazing support system when Steve was sick, and after he died. My family has always been there for me every moment of my life. I am who I am because of them. My family has been and still is a major help. Not only do they help me with my sons and fixing things at my house, but they support me in prayer. When I go through periods of depression, I feel my spirit being lifted as a result of their prayers.

My mother-in-law was a huge blessing to me. My mother in law was a widow at age 33. Her husband died from the same disease my husband died from twenty years apart. My mother in law buried her husband and her son, my God! She could have easily given up, but she didn't. When she lost her husband, she raised her children to become three of the greatest people I know. She took care of my husband the first time he was sick. When he died, she was there for me. When I think of her I think about Naomi. She is my Naomi and I am her Ruth. My mother-in-law has a special place in my heart because she understands what it is like to be a young widow. After Steve passed, she was able to help me with things that no one else understood. She was an angel that God sent to be with me in the midst of tragedy. Even though God allowed tragedy to occur, He never left me alone.

When I tell you that God has overwhelmed me with his love, it is an understatement. My family has been and still is a major help. Not only do they help me with my sons and fixing things at my house, but they also help me by praying. I get depressed and sometimes it is bad. I do not know how I am going to go on. Then I start feeling my spirit being lifted-that is the result of their prayers and support. God has sent me a great group of friends and co workers as well. There is so much love around me it is insane. God placed family, friends, church family and co-workers around me to help me with my sons as well. There are people praying for me even as I wrote this book.

Of course there has been some changes. Some friendships changed and that was hard. What I now understand is that God sends you exactly what you need when you need it. He does not eliminate people from your life with no reason, He just readjusts the role that person plays in your life. There were some friendships that changed significantly for me. I'll be honest, it did hurt. It felt like another loss. Over time and with prayer I was able to see a different perspective. When someone close is removed from your life, He will provide other people and resources to help you.

Truth #4: God Wants You to be Honest about Your Pain

This is where we get tripped up. We don't talk to God about the pain He allowed. We hold it in, which leads to resentment towards God. I remember being in a season where I could not pray, read my word or fast. I didn't trust God. I had to get to the root of the problem. The reason why I did not trust God is because I trusted God when my husband was sick and God allowed him to die! That's real disappointment! My grandmother used to have a saying: Fool me ONCE, shame on YOU. Fool me TWICE shame on ME. That is how I felt about God. He fooled me once when I trusted Him fully, He is not going to fool me again! So I struggled (and sometimes still do) with fully trusting God. Fear is the root of my trust issues. I am afraid to trust Him fully because of what He may allow. Remember I trusted Him with my husband's life; He allowed him to die. So now when faced with a problem, I struggle because I fear that God will allow more pain. So I pray daily (because I am supposed to) and still work on trying to fix every problem. I say this present tense because I still go through periods of this. It is draining and absurd. I know better and when you know better, you do better! The reality is I am human. This walk with God is truly a journey. There are many highs and lows. There is light and darkness. The pain is REAL!

Before moving on I need to address something. God gives us free will. What that means is that God gives us the ability to think for ourselves and decide whether we want to follow Him or not. Some of our pain comes from our own choices, but He allows it. In order to heal from pain and trust God through the unimaginable you must have some accountability. You must be held accountable for your part in your pain if your actions played a part. God is not limited to space or time so He already knows what decision you will make. He will even use the pain that you brought upon yourself to bless you and others! He is just awesome in that way!

The Pain of Disappointment

In addition to the pain of loss and death, I also had to face the pain of disappointment from the God I always believed would comfort me, protect me, and provide for me. When He allowed Steve to die, it felt like a betrayal at first.

What do you do when God disappoints you? When you prayed and believed God for something and it did not work out the way you wanted. Maybe you didn't get the job you really wanted or the person you are interested in does not feel the same way. Maybe the disappointment is deeper – perhaps you were believing God for a clean bill of health and instead you got a terminal diagnosis. Or, you were believing God for reconciliation and He allowed the relationship to end.

Disappointment is no joke. I remember the disappointment I felt when the doctor said that Steve would need a second lung transplant after the double lung transplant he received in 2011. We waited for months and endured countless hospital visits before the call we prayed for came on May 1, 2012. We were actually on our way home from the hospital when we got the news that there was a donor. We turned around immediately, full of hope, and said many prayers with Steve as he went into surgery.

As my family and I sat waiting for the surgery to be over, I thought about the opportunity for our lives to begin again after his recovery. I daydreamed about us having another baby, something we talked about. I believed God had answered our prayers and that I was in the midst of a miracle.

Two hours into the procedure, the surgeon came out and delivered a bombshell – they found an issue with the donor lungs and they could not perform the transplant. They had to wake Steve up to let him know that he did not actually have a transplant and that we were back to where we started. Even with this news, I remember encouraging myself to remain positive and hopeful. I kept telling myself that God's will is perfect and we would get another call. When several weeks passed with no call, the word disappointed doesn't begin to describe what I was feeling. What was the point of all of that praying and believing? I felt like God was playing with us. I felt like he teased us by getting our hopes up and letting it down all in a day. Steve died two months later.

The truth is, I will never understand why God allowed this sequence of events, and that is okay. What I have learned is that we may never understand what God does. Some things that God allows cannot be explained; they are not meant for us to understand. That is where our faith and trust in God must be our solace. We have to trust God even when we do not understand or like what He is doing.

Proverbs 3:5-6 tells us, "*Trust in the Lord with all your heart, do not depend on your own understanding*[6] *Seek his will in all you do, and he will show you which path to take."*

In this scripture God doesn't promise us that we will always understand, he plainly tells us not to rely on our own understanding. He tells us to focus on him and trust him. My heart was crushed when Steve's transplant did not work out. It would have been very easy to become bitter. In fact, it took more work to be positive than it would have to remained negative. I began to silently question if God really was real. Did he really hear my prayers? Did he really care about me? I experienced the pain of disappointment again with loosing my mom.

My mom passed away suddenly at age 53. Our family was devastated. I was angry with God again! Not only was the fact that she died devastating but the manner in which she died hurt as well. I remember her calling me that Friday night. We talked like we always did and hung up. Noting out of the ordinary. The next afternoon my sister called me. As soon as I saw her name on the phone, I did not have a good feeling for some reason. My mom was very sick. She had many health challenges over the years but never something like this.

My mom ended up passing away a few days later. My mom was way too young to die in my opinion. She had a lot of life still in her. I remember her stopping what she was doing to come stay with me for weeks at a time when Steve was sick. I remember her staying with me after he died for a while as well. We had gotten so close and I was so happy about that. I needed my mother. My siblings and I are in our 20s & 30s, we all still needed her. My sons needed their grandmother.

I remember explaining to my older son that God chose to heal her eternally. I had this same conversation with him about my husband. I explained that sometimes God heals people here on Earth and sometimes Heaven is where they receive healing. I remember him asking, "Why does God always let our family go to Heaven? Why doesn't he heal them here?" I had some questions for God myself. Why was he torturing us? This was cruel and unfair! I just didn't get why my mom would be taken so suddenly. It was just unfair! I felt like I was a magnet for pain. My mother's death took the breath out of me, yet God was still right there with me. Because my mom loved the Lord, I knew she was with him. That and the fact that I knew she wasn't suffering was comforting. The disappointment and pain was still all too real.

The Pain of Rejection

There is another area of pain that can make us question if God cares about us. That area is rejection. This area is hard for me to discuss because rejection is a deep rooted pain. I even struggled about whether I should share my pain in this area. I was going to leave it out, but I must be obedient to what God leads me to write. Long before I met Steve, I battle overwhelming feelings of rejection. I felt like I was not good enough. I was so desperate for the approval of others that rejection (or perceived rejection) was an agonizing pain. I actually did not live with my mom growing up, I lived with my dad. My mom and siblings lived close by and we saw each other regularly. For me, I had such a low self esteem growing up and the root was all based on a perceived (not real) rejection. I thought that the reason I did not live with my mom was because she did not want me. I spent so much time believing this lie that I ignored signs that said otherwise. Looking back now, I wish I would have asked her about it. I wish I wouldn't have made so many assumptions and just got the facts. Because I was the only child that did not live with her, I just assumed that there was something wrong with me. I did not see how hard my mom tried to connect with me. I did not see how sometimes the problem was me and not her. Sometimes I didn't reach out or receive the love she was offering. A relationship involves two parties. I was not always doing my part.

Sometimes I focused on what she didn't do instead of all that she did. I just believed the lie that the enemy told me which was I was unwanted and unloved, all lies! My mom loved me so much! Now that I am a parent, I realize how hard it is to give your kids what they need. I realized how different the needs of your children are. I try to give both Quincy and Kevin what they need and sometimes I miss the mark. Sometimes one child gets more of me than the other. The reality is I am human and flawed. I will not always get it right. This is why the grace of God is so real, it picks up where I slack off. My mom was with me during one of the hardest times of my life. She stayed with me when Steve was sick. She could've been anywhere else but she was right there. So the fact that I didn't see her daily did not take away from the fact that she was still a good mom. My mom was not perfect but she did the best she could and for that I am so thankful. Perceived rejection took away years that I could have spent bonding with my mother. It also took away years that I could have lived feeling loved because I was just that, I was loved.

Rejection has been a part of my life for as long as I can remember. I often felt misunderstood as a kid. I never could quite articulate how I truly felt and I was an expert at faking like I was happy. I performed well in school and most people thought I was just another kid. I was dying slowly inside and no one knew. I desperately wanted to be accepted, to be loved. I experienced the rejection of friends and when I was old enough to date, it got worse. I didn't fit in.

I tried so hard to be like everyone else but I just wasn't. No one knew how desperate I was for acceptance. No one knew about the suicide thoughts and attempts. It seemed like whenever I got close to someone, something changed. I either moved or for some reason, that relationship ended. The anxiety was overwhelming. The low self esteem was slowly killing my spirit. People never knew what was behind my smile. I never got that approval I was so desperate for. I am still often misunderstood and even talked about. Rejection or perceived rejection has been a challenge. I believed the lie that the enemy told me. The enemy said I was unwanted and a nuisance. The enemy said I wasn't good enough. Looking back, I wonder how much of the rejection that I felt was real, or just a lie from the enemy.

One lie from the enemy led me to a lifetime of feeling rejected and unwanted. Romans 8: 6 says, *"The mind governed by the flesh is death, the mind governed by the spirit is life and peace."* Sometimes the pain we feel is based on what we think and not what we know. Guard your mind! I have thought myself into depression before. The word of God tells us to take every thought captive. That is not to say my pain was not real or valid, but my thoughts and choice to believe the lies the enemy told did not make things better. The mind is such an amazing creation. The ability to remember the past, process the present and dream of the future all at the same time is absolutely amazing. On the other end, when there is pain involved, the mind can be challenging. One simple thought can take us right back to that place of pain. Have you ever heard a song and it instantly takes you back? It took months before I could listen to "You & I" by Stevie Wonder as that was our wedding song. A song that use to make me cry tears of joy now made me cry tears of agony. Guarding our mind is key especially when God's will takes us down a road that we didn't expect.

The Comparison Trap

Sometimes, pain makes us feel like we are the only ones hurting. We may feel like someone else's pain is not as significant as ours. I remember someone talking to me about another young widow and they said, "You know, Whitney, your husband was sick but this woman has it worse, her husband died suddenly!" Although I cannot fathom the pain of losing a loved one suddenly, it is heartbreaking to have to watch the one you love lose their life slowly. Here is the deal: pain is pain. There is no pain more significant than the other.

God does not triage our pain. If you are in pain of any kind, it is valid and it matters to Him. Everyone's pain is equally important in His eyes, and He is waiting to bring healing and comfort. Be careful not to minimize someone else's pain; resist the temptation to compare your pain to theirs. Instead, when others are hurting, walk with them. Seek ways to be a blessing to them and meet their needs.

The truth is things can occur and hurt so badly that you question if God is real. God is indeed real and if you thought the pain was a lot to take in, get ready for the promises!

Promises

*'He will wipe every tear from their eyes. There will be no more death' or mourning or crying or **pain**, for the old order of things has passed away."*
Revelation 21:4

There is a reason God gave me this book title. We spend so much time focusing on our pain that we easily forget about the promises of God. It can be hard to see the good God has for you when your heart is shattered. When I think back to 2012 and I look at all that has happened to me since then, no one can convince me that God is not real. I went through so many devastating circumstances – losing my husband, becoming a single mom, and learning to meet the needs of my son diagnosed with autism, all while managing school, work and home was overwhelming at times. However, God has shown me so much mercy.

It has been nearly five years since my husband died, and God allowed me to buy my first home, fulfill my passion to become a special education teacher, earn three post-secondary degrees, and be healed and restored to a place where I can minister to others and share my story through this book. My boys are doing wonderfully. While we are far from perfect, God has shown us abundant favor. That is just who God is!

Just as there are truths we need to recognize when it comes to our pain, there are also truths we should recognize when it comes to God's promises.

Truth #1: The Promises Outweigh The Pain

Sounds cliché, right? It's not! Our pain is temporary, but the promises of God are forever! While God's promises do not take away the sting of the pain, they are our hope that God will be with us to carry us through it and use it to mold us, shape us and teach us. There is nothing wrong with acknowledging the reality of our pain; disappointing circumstances are something that none of us would wish on ourselves. Losing a spouse is not easy, but God showed me through my painful situation just who He made me to be.

2 Corinthians 1: 20 tells us, *"For all of God's promises have been fulfilled in Christ with a resounding "Yes!" And through Christ, our "Amen" (which means "Yes") ascends to God for his glory."*

What does this mean? It means that ALL of God's promises are met with a YES! He withholds nothing from us! If He has a promise for your life it will happen! For every pain we have God also has a promise. Your pain is not in vain, I promise! When my husband died, God made me a promise. He promised me that my boys and I would be okay. He has kept his promise. My boys and I have been more than okay. We have not been perfect, but He never promised me that. He promised me that our needs would be met and that He would be with us. That He has done. He has sent angels to enter our lives and remind us that we are covered. No matter what we have endured it will never compare to the promises God has for us.

Romans 8:18 says, *"Yet what we suffer now is nothing compared to the glory he will reveal to us later."*

The suffering will occur but not without the glory! Never doubt that!

You may be in for the fight of your life right now. You may feel like there are wars in every area and you can't catch a break. You may actually be in for the fight of your life but understand this: the fight is fixed! You have already won! I do not care how it looks or feels right now, you are victorious! I know that may sound so cliché but it is oh so true.

Many of us have heard the story of David & Goliath, but we often do not stop and think about the odds David was up against. Goliath was over nine feet tall and he was undefeated against the Israelites; there was no one courageous enough to face him. It would have been logical for God to allow an army to finally take Goliath down, but He used David – a young shepherd boy with no previous military experience.

That is the funny thing about how God operates, He puts us in impossible situations only to prove them possible through Him. David was unqualified by man's standards but for God, he was the man for the job. Goliath thought it was comical when He saw David coming! Clearly it was no competition.

What I love about David is what he says to Goliath just before the battle.

He says in 1 Samuel 12: 45-46, *"David replied to the Philistine, "You come to me with sword, spear, and javelin, but I come to you in the name of the Lord of Heaven's Armies—the God of of Israel, whom you have defied. Today the Lord will conquer you, and I will kill you and cut off your head. And then I will give the dead bodies of your men to the birds and wild animals, and the whole world will know that there is a God in Israel!"*

What confidence in God! God used David to kill Goliath in the end. Even though David seemed the least prepared to defeat a giant, his faith and confidence in God led him to experience victory What if we spoke to the Goliath in our life the way David did?

God promises that He will fight our battles for us, no matter how big they are, and we will be victorious. I've heard the saying, "Sometimes God will put a Goliath in your life for you to find the David within you" and I definitely believe it. What is our response to the giants that we have to face? Do we cower in fear and uncertainty, or stand strong and declare God's promises?

Sometimes the pain is so great that we begin to think that pain is God's plan for our lives. We think that it is God's will for us to always endure pain and that life will not get better. That is not true at all! God wants us to have an abundant life! He wants you to have a prosperous life! Although I have endured tremendous loss, God has provided tremendous blessings! He has made ways out of no ways. He has supplied all that I needed and more. He has breathed fresh life into my body and new hope into my heart. God showed me that even in tragedy he would still fulfill his promises! The promises outweigh the pain! The promises of God are not just tangible items, what He does for your heart is much greater, but you must believe.

Truth #2: The Pain Positions You for the Promises

God has so much more for you, beyond what you can see. He knows how much you have suffered. He has seen the pain, the heartache, the tears, the loss, the sleepless nights, etc. He has not abandoned or forgotten you in any way. When our pain is heaviest, that is often when God positions us to rely on Him like never before. If you allow the Word of God to be the hope that you hold onto in the midst of your pain, His promises will bring healing.

During the first few months after Steve died, I did not know to do. I was trying to care for my kids, work and go to school full time. My emotions were all over the place. However, I found that God's Word addressed every feeling. My favorite chapter of the bible is Romans 8. I love the entire chapter. Whenever I am feeling low, that chapter is my go-to. There are so many powerful scriptures in this chapter. When you are going through something, look up scriptures on that topic. Allow God's Word to wash over you and pull you out of that dark place.

Truth #3: The Promises of God Reveal the Love of God

We can't talk about the promises of God without talking about the love of God. God's love is like no other love; it gets us through the toughest times. I remember the nights I would lay in bed and just cry. At times, the physical & emotional pain of my grief was so severe that I literally felt like I was in labor. During those times, I would cry out to God and beg Him to ease the pain; in His loving mercy, He honored those prayers. While I cannot articulate into words what He did, I could feel His tangible presence in those moments. He brought calm to my body and eased my mind. He helped me rest and His love equipped me to live another day.

The love of God is that instant comfort that comes to you. It is freeing, it is poetic; it is how God shows us He is real. Even though your pain may be unbearable, it does not compare to the love of God (Romans 8:18). God loves us so much that He removed the greatest pain from us-the cross. All the pain in the world does not compare to what Jesus endured on the cross. Although God allows tremendous pain at times, He loved us enough to save us from the greatest pain. What a loving God! Sometimes, you have to thank God for the pain He didn't allow!

Once we encounter the love of God, we are never the same. God's love heals, repairs and restores. The word of God tells us that the love of God covers a multitude of sins, and I believe it covers a multitude of pain as well.

Truth #4: The Promises of God Change Us

The promises of God change us; when we experience God's presence in a personal way, we are not the same as we were before that experience. Ephesians 2 compares the character of someone before they accept God's promise of salvation to after they invite God to take control of their lives.

Ephesians 2:1-3 says,
"As for you, you were dead in your transgressions and sins, [2] in which you used to live when you followed the ways of this world and of the ruler of the kingdom of the air, the spirit who is now at work in those who are disobedient. [3] All of us also lived among them at one time, gratifying the cravings of our flesh[a] and following its desires and thoughts. Like the rest, we were by nature deserving of wrath."

If we read further, we will see that our imperfect past is not our final destination. The passage goes on to say in verses 4-7, *"⁴ But because of his great love for us, God, who is rich in mercy, ⁵ made us alive with Christ even when we were dead in transgressions—it is by grace you have been saved. ⁶ And God raised us up with Christ and seated us with him in the heavenly realms in Christ Jesus, ⁷ in order that in the coming ages he might show the incomparable riches of his grace, expressed in his kindness to us in Christ Jesus."*

God's presence is transformative. Many times, He will use our pain to develop stronger character in us. Think about your life before a certain tragedy or disappointment occurred. How were you living? How did what you experienced impact your relationship with God? If you felt like God had forsaken you or was punishing you, I encourage you to read through Ephesians 2 and ask God to remind you of His love, the riches of His grace, and His kindness. Allow Him to comfort you and give you a new perspective.

No matter where we came from or what sin is stored up in our past, God has raised us up; that is His promise. By His grace we are saved! No matter how much the pain broke you, God has raised you up! When we give our lives to Him, His promise of salvation is fulfilled. He will heal you through your situation. His promises never return void.

Truth #5: The promises of God   position you to tell the goodness of God.

Your pain is not about you. It is an opportunity for you to grow, learn, and encourage someone else with the story of how God delivered you. God will strategically align you to the people who need to hear your testimony. When the time comes, do not hold back. Tell your story in its entirety and allow God to minister to that person. If you feel like your story is not valuable because it is not "pretty" and perfect, you are wrong – your story is beautiful and purposeful. Never doubt your value to God and to His people. Be bold in telling people the whole truth of what God has done in your life. There are people who may have seen your struggle and now they see your promise. Or there are people who see your promise but don't know your struggle. This is the time to open your mouth and tell everyone who will listen what God has done.

I grew up wishing that I had the perfect story. I wanted to go straight to college, marry my high school sweetheart, have three kids, have a wonderful home and just be happy. My life has not been the way I planned, to say the least, but it has been the way God has planned. That is the beauty of the promises of God; they are uniquely beautiful. Even though I do not have the story I envisioned for my life, it is indeed beautiful. You have to learn to see the goodness of God even in a dark place.

I love when people tell me how strong I am. Not because I want to hear about me, but because it is an opportunity to tell them how great God is. I love sharing where I have come from and what God has done for me. Four months before Steve died, I completed an associate's degree. I had started my bachelor's degree and was three weeks into my first semester when Steve passed. Through God's grace, I have now completed my bachelors and a master's degree all the while taking care of my boys. I am in no way bragging, all the credit belongs to God! He promised me that the boys and I would be okay. We are more than okay; we are favored! I do not ever want to give off the impression that I have it all together. When you see me, you see the grace of God. I have no problem sharing that. God has positioned angels around us and has strengthened us to share our testimony with others.

Truth #6: God Wants His Promises to Flow through You to Others

One of the most beautiful realities is that the promises of God are not just for you. The promises God has for you will not just bless you but it will bless those you love. I believe that the promises God has for me will bless my family for generations to come. God desires not only for you to be free, but for your family and those who connect with you to be healed and have joy also.

2 Peter 1: 4 says, *"4 Through these he has given us his very great and precious promises, so that through them you may participate in the divine nature, having escaped the corruption in the world caused by evil desires."*

I had to believe that God not only had promises for me but more importantly promises for my children as well. My children have been through so much! My older son is simply amazing in my eyes. He has endured so much (I am believing God that he will share his own testimony someday) yet still does well in school, is a great help at home and has many great gifts and talents. I could not be more proud of him. I have prayed over him and I trust that God's promises apply to his life as well. My younger son, who was diagnosed with autism, is defying the odds. I remember being told that he would not speak. He is now reading! He has overcome obstacle after obstacle and does it with a smile.

Truth #7: Your Promise Must Be Rooted in God's Word

Sometimes we are waiting for things that are not coming. Why? Because God did not promise them! God did not promise you a mate who is already taken, or mate who does not love Him. He did not promise you a promotion that you have to compromise yourself to get and He did not promise you money you did not earn honestly. Again, if your promise cannot be traced to the word of God, it is not from Him. We have to us what we know about God's character and His ultimate purpose for our lives to discern if something that comes to our lives is a blessing, or just a distraction.

I believe that God promised me that I will remarry. A few years after Steve died, I met a guy that I really grew to like. I had not met anyone prior to that and it was nice to meet someone totally new. He came at a time that I was not looking. We had so much in common and he was not intimidated by my story. On my own, I decided that this was the man God promised for me; I didn't even bother to pray.

It turned out that this man not who God called me to be with. How did I know? God sent me several warnings signs. Because our friendship caused me to drift away from God instead of drawing me closer. I started to compromise myself to be more interesting to him. I started loosening up my beliefs to make him feel comfortable. Honestly, when I look back on that time, I am still embarrassed. Steve was an upstanding gentleman who loved and respected me. He did not play games or play with my feelings. He made his intentions clear and sent no mixed signals. Why was I entertaining someone who was doing the exact opposite? I know what God promised me – why was I settling? The truth is it felt good to be thought of. It felt good to have someone to talk to. It felt good to meet a new person. It was very hard to break away. I knew I needed to separate myself from this person. It took some time for me to end that friendship but once I did, I felt free. I literally blocked their number and never looked back. I deserved better. I spent time healing and seeking forgiveness and now I am positioned (free from clutter) so that God can fulfill the promise in my life for that area. I had to let go of the clutter to make room for the promise. Here are a few promises that we can believe for, based on the Word of God.

The Promise of Healing

Jeremiah 30:17 says,

*"But I will restore you to health and heal your wounds,'
declares the LORD, 'because you are called an
outcast, Zion for whom no one cares."*

God will heal all of your wounds and restore you totally. You may feel like your pain has isolated you from others. Being a young widow made me feel isolated, as did being a mom of a child with autism. Yet through all of this, God still restored me. Often, the enemy would trick me into believing that God did not care about me because if He did care, He would not have allowed so much tragedy to happen to me. The truth is that although God allows the pain, He also orchestrates the restoration. The pain may have isolated you. There may be people who were once vital to your life who are now distant. You may even feel like the walls are closing in on you. No matter how lonely you feel, take comfort in knowing that the God we serve is omnipresent. He is always with you. The breath of fresh air that soothes you is Him. That song that comes on at the right time with right lyrics is Him. That post online that speaks directly to you is Him. The phone call from a friend with a word of encouragement is Him. The will to get out of the bed and start a new day is Him. The grace to still handle everything despite a broken heart is Him.

The Promise of Protection

One of the things the Lord promises us is His protection. *Psalm 68:5 says, "A father to the fatherless, a defender of widows is God in his holy dwelling."* When my husband died, I wondered about protection and provision. Who would cover us like my husband did? Who would help my boys? I know that I am a strong woman and great mother but I cannot teach my boys to be men. I cannot be a father to my youngest son because God made me a mother. I know the value of a man of God, and my boys lost one of the greatest men I had ever known.

God's promises are true, He is indeed a defender of the widow. He has made sure that myself and my boys lacked nothing. He has aligned angels to intercept when the boys and I had a need. He has sent Godly men in the form of family, friends, mentors and church family to be present in my boys' lives. I think of my youngest son particularly. My older son still has his father and his family, but Kevin's father, paternal grandfather and maternal grandmother are no longer here. Kevin will never know what it is like to have a father/son relationship. Steve never got to see Kevin start school. He did not get to see all the progress Kevin has made and how autism is not defining his life. While this makes me sad, Psalm 68:5 gives me hope. God is not only a defender of widows; He is also a father to the fatherless. Although Kevin's earthly father is not here, his heavenly Father is always here. God is a void filler, even when the void is the loss of a father. There will never be a man to replace Stephen, but our heavenly father will fill every void for both of my boys. God is a defender and protector to all who love Him! Rest in the fact that He has your best interest at heart, even when it does not seem like it.

One hard part about the protection and defending that God does for His people is that we do not always get to see the manifestation of justice. Right now our country is in a critical state. Racism and injustice is at an all time high. Every time I turn around there are unarmed black men, women and teens being brutally murdered. I sit in horror as I watch in many instances these deaths fade away without justice. I often lay awake and ask God,

"Where is their protection? Where is their justice?" I wish I could give you this wonderful answer that makes it all better but I cannot. What I can say is that God always defends His children. Anyone who comes against God's children will be subject to His wrath. So even though some offenders do not get the justice that I want to see, God will hold them accountable for their actions in the end. Sometimes we do not see all the promises of God, but we have to trust that He will bring every single one to completion.

The Promise of Eternal Life

One of the most beautiful aspects of the promises of God is the ultimate promise of eternal life. Salvation is a gift and the ultimate demonstration of God's love for us. No matter how much pain you are in, know that it has an expiration date. If you have accepted Christ as your personal Savior then you know and believe that even after this life is over, you will still live. The promises of God are eternal! No matter what you endure during this life, there is a day when your pain will end. Even death cannot stop the promises of God. Sometimes when I am feeling low, I dream of Heaven. A place where there is no illness, no sadness, no lack. I dream of my loved ones who are already there. I dream of the beauty of Heaven. Knowing that once my life ends here, I will awaken to see the face of God, instantly gives me hope to go on another day.

Expecting, Waiting and Receiving

The promises of God often come to us through a three-phase process: expecting, waiting and receiving. Expecting may seem simple, but it can be difficult. Do you expect the promises of God in your life? Do you truly believe that God will do it? I would love to say that I truly believed that God would bring about His promises for my life when Steve died, but I did not. I expected pain. I expected lack. I expected tragedy. I did not expect abundance. I did not expect healing. I did not expect favor. What we expect is what we yield to our lives. If we expect pain, we get it. If we expect joy, we get it. Even in our most difficult moments, we need to expect God to show up, and He will. Walk today and every day with expectation that you will see the promises of God in your life, and position yourself to receive them. It is our expectation that keeps us strong (Psalm 27:13-14).

Expecting and believing in your heart that God has promises for you is one thing; waiting on the promises of God is another. I will be the first to say that patience is not my area of strength. I hate waiting, especially I do not know what I am waiting for or when it will come.

Romans 8:25 says (New Living Translation), "But if we look forward to something we don't yet have, we must wait patiently and confidently."

What does this mean? It means we must be patient, yet expectant, when waiting on the promises of God. This is yet another reason why reading the Word of God is so important. When the waiting is long, you need the word of God to fill you with trust and hope. If it seems like you are waiting forever, or you are running out of time, remember that God is intentional. He is not bound to time, space or any other circumstances.

44

Receiving the promises of God is the moment we have been waiting for. I cannot imagine the joy Sarah felt holding Isaac for the first time (Genesis 21: 1-3). She waited 90 years for that moment. I am sure that there were many dark days during that time when she that she worried if God heard her prayers. However, the day came when she held Isaac for the first time, her promise became reality.

Do not spend your time idly waiting for God to move. The best thing you can do while waiting is to prepare and praise Him in advance. Remember someone is always watching you, let them see you praise even in the midst of your storm.

You might wonder how I can possibly write about expecting promises of God after experiencing so much disappointment in my life. However, that is the exact reason that I need to share my story – God's promises are always "yes," even though the realization of His promises often do not come in the way we think they should. Even today, I still have to go through the process of expecting, waiting and receiving.

I still never know how God will intervene in my life. I wish I could tell you the day that all the repairs in my house will be fixed or the day when my finances will be favorable. I wish I could share the exact day when I will meet my future husband or when my children will receive certain miracles, but I can't. However, I choose to trust God because I know that the only way I will make it through any storm is through His power and with His guidance. Going through storms with God is much more bearable than going through without Him.

What promise are you believing God for today? Your promise from God may not be something tangible. It may be deliverance, emotional healing, freedom, or favor. Whatever it is, the moment God breathes life into it is amazing.

When we receive a promise from God, it is important to stay humble and grounded, always giving Him the glory. Sometimes we get to the promise and forget that it was God, not our own wisdom, that carried us through the struggle. When you share your testimony, be sure that you always give God the credit He deserves.

Process

***I press on** toward the goal to win the prize for which God has called me heavenward in Christ Jesus.*
Philippians 3:14

So, we have talked about the pain and God's promises, but how is it possible to go from being devastated to trusting God again? I can assure you that it does not happen overnight; there is a process. I will be honest, I use to hate the word process. I wanted immediate healing, provision and favor. If I can be really transparent, I felt entitled to it; I felt that God owed me. Since he took my husband, the least he could do was make sure the rest of my life was problem- free. I had a lot to learn; that is not how God works. He takes us through various processes to strengthen us. I love the analogy of the diamond. The diamond is molded and sculpted into the beauty we see. The diamond is the final result; the process is the sculpting. The diamond is a diamond from the beginning; the process just makes it more beautiful and stronger. We must endure the ugly stage to embrace the beauty of our diamond. Similarly, we are already victorious in Christ; the process just makes us stronger and our light brighter, so that we attract more people to Him. What does the process entail? It is different for all of us. I have broken the process down into six phases: Realization, Acceptance, Perspective, Restoration, Forgiveness, and Dismantling Fear.

Phase #1: Realization

In the realization phase, you need a moment to catch your breath and take in what has occurred. It is important to remember that your feelings are valid and God cares about you. When Steve died, I needed a moment to process. A good friend of mine paid for me to spend the night alone in a hotel shortly after the funeral. I was so excited to have a night to myself, kid free. My house had been full with family and I desperately needed alone time. However, when I got the information about my hotel stay, my heart sank. My friend unknowingly got me a room at the hotel I stayed in for my wedding night. That night, it got real between God and I. I cried and screamed at him. I was devastated, mad, sad, heartbroken and confused. The reality had hit me that Steve was gone, and the fear of the unknown began to develop. How was I going to feed my sons and complete school? How would I support my youngest son who was newly diagnosed with autism? How would I do it all?

A lot of times as Christians, we try to short change this part of the process. We don't want to face that dark place. What is worse is that we are afraid to be that vulnerable. We do not want people to see us in that state. We want people to see us as that strong man or woman of God that never doubts, never breaks and always trusts God. Isn't that the person who shows up on Sundays? Isn't that the person who posts nothing but positive things on social media? We don't want people to see that we are hurting deeply, because we are afraid of being judged.

The length of the process is different for everyone. Sometimes, we think it is over and then God stretches us even more. About six months after Steve died, another event occur that almost took away every bit of faith that I had left.

My pediatrician suggested that I have Kevin see a pulmonary specialist. He was concerned because Steve and his father died from the same lung disease and he wanted Kevin to be checked. I did not like the fact that I had to take Kevin back to the same hospital that I went to with my husband, but everything appeared to be fine. After several months of check-ups, the doctor suggested doing a CT scan of his lungs as a final measure before discontinuing his appointments.

It was all good until I got the phone call that Kevin's CT scan came back abnormal, they had found "something" on his lungs. I lost it - how dare God do this? Kevin had just turned four; wasn't losing his dad and having autism enough? Were we about to have to go through this heart wrenching agony again? I felt like God had gone too far. I remember threatening God; I remember saying thing like, "You better not let my son get sick!" or "I'm done serving you!" I do not curse, but I am sure I dropped a few choice words then. I was tired and I was furious.

The wonderful part about the God I serve is that He loves us through it all! He could have left me in my moments of anger and frustration, but He didn't. He could have punished me, but He didn't. Instead He comforted me. When I felt I couldn't take any more, He clothed me with His peace. He gave me the strength to get through the doctor appointments, bronchoscopy, and more CT scans. He comforted me when I cried myself to sleep. He loved even when I lashed out at Him. He allowed me to be vulnerable and authentic during my realization process. When tragedy happens and you feel like you have been hit, I encourage you go to God – pray a raw prayer and give Him your pain.

Phase #2: Acceptance

After realization, the next phase is acceptance. Acceptance has many layers. First, you need to simply accept what has happened. I had to accept that the love of my life had died. I was now a widow; my children lost a parent. That is a hard pill to swallow. Secondly, you need to accept that what happened was God's will. After much agony and tears, God brought me to accept that although He heard all of my prayers and everyone else's prayers, it was still His will for Steve to die. I needed to accept that this was God's answer.

Acceptance does not mean that you understand or are okay with what has happened; it simply means that you are at peace with it. This phase takes time; acceptance requires a ton of prayer and support from others within the body of Christ. For some, counseling may also be of help. Contrary to what some people think, counseling does not mean that you do not trust God. In fact, God can speak through counselors. I have been to counseling off and on my entire life. When Steve died, I ran to a grief counseling group that my church offered. It was so refreshing to be directed to passages of scripture that spoke to my feelings. It was also nice to meet people who were on similar journeys. I also did one-on-one counseling (and still do), which has helped me peel back layers of pain. It does not matter what unique process God takes you through to reach acceptance, as long as you get there.

Phase #3: Perspective

Perspective is the next phase of the process. During this phase, God changes your mind and heart; it is amazing! This phase requires heavy time in God's Word and deep prayer. I will admit, I will pray all day every day, but sometimes reading my word is hard. Sometimes it feels like a chore to me, which is insane because I love God and I love to read. As hard as it can be to carve out that time to read, it is essential in the process. I am not talking about quoting your favorite scripture or a quick minute devotional. Those are wonderful, but they will not sustain you. To truly allow God to change your perspective you have to dig deep into your Word, allow God to speak to you through the scriptures, and listen for His direction.

About a month before Steve died, I began reading and studying the book of Job. I just knew that Steve was like Job. I focused on how Job was a good man and how he got double for his trouble in the end (I suggest you read Job in depth because is much more to his story). Some of our close friends even did a fast for Steve's healing, based on scripture.

Psalm 118:17, "Therefore I will not die but live and proclaim what the Lord has done."

I remember having these scriptures in my head as I was leaving the hospital on July 4, 2012. That morning I received the call that Steve was on life support. I stayed with him all day but finally went to be with my kids. My mind knew it was the end but my heart wasn't ready. I remember laying awake that night and crying out to God. I remember saying to God, "Why did you have me reading about Job if Steve was going to die? Why are you torturing me!" I laid on the floor of my aunt's basement that night and wept. I finally said angrily, "God, you're a joke. Had me reading that scripture about not dying. Steve is clearly dying!" Then, at that moment, God spoke four words that changed my perspective. I distinctly heard "It wasn't for him."

God was telling me those scriptures were for *me*, not Steve. The book of Job was meant to encourage me. God wanted me to put my name into Psalm 118:17. Whitney will not die but will live and proclaim what the Lord has done. My mind was blown away in that moment. God already knew what was going to happen, He led me to those scriptures to prepare me. What an amazing God!

Initially, I felt that God did not answer my prayers. However, God changed my perspective and reminded me of His promise in Mark 11:24 which says, "*Whatever you ask for in prayer, believe that you will receive it, and it will be yours.*" I prayed for Steve to be healed, and God answered, even though it was much differently than what I expected and wanted. Steve is eternally healed; he will never have an ounce of illness again.

God was purposeful in Steve's life and death, and he showed me that even death has a purpose.

Someone got saved at Steve's funeral. People made life altering decisions after Steve died. Some family members gave their lives back to God after he died. Both his life and death had purpose. When God first laid that thought on my heart, I did not want to receive it at first, but it is the truth.

The perspective is tough, but so necessary. Once you allow God to change your perspective, you experience a level of freedom that is indescribable. Changing your perspective does not magically take away the pain. It just helps to give you a different frame of mind and, most importantly, it helps you maintain your peace.

Perspective requires you to change your speech. What are you saying? Are you speaking life or death? As Steve's health declined, he was unable to communicate. Imagine a minister who did not have enough oxygen to speak! Whenever he spoke, he had to be short and direct. He did not have enough oxygen to waste breaths complaining, being mean or negative. He used his last breaths to praise God and encourage others. He always managed to crack a joke. I often correct myself. When I am stressed I begin complaining and whining. Steve did not waste oxygen being negative, I must do the same! I must use my words to speak life. When you are enduring the process to healing after tragedy, you must speak life. Be mindful of what you say and what you allow around you.

Phase #4: Restoration

Restoration is when you get your life back. Restoration is when God gives you a breath of fresh air. It is during this time that you experience an overwhelming sense of peace. During the restoration phase you can reflect on what has happened. During this phase you take your life back and new beginnings occur. It took me a few years to get to the restoration phase after Steve died. I finally got to a place where I took my life back. I was not just Steve's widow; I became Whitney again. I started traveling some and spending time with my girlfriends. I even started going out by myself from time to time. Life was no longer just going through the motions, I actually started living.

Restoration is a wonderful time to reflect. As I look back on 2012, I am simply in awe of God. I recall at how devastated I was back then; I used to think that life would never get better. I thought that I could not live without Steve. As I look at the multiple miracles that God performed during that time, I have clear evidence that through God, I can overcome anything.

There is no quick fix in any part of the process. If you want the healing, you have to do the work. It can take days, months or even years. It is not a fun process either. This is the time to be raw and authentic. I spoke previously of having raw conversations with God. You cannot endure the process without it.

Phase #5: Forgiveness

Forgiveness is another part of the process. If your devastation is due to pain caused by another person, you need to ask God to help you forgive that person. Sometimes, we think that people do not deserve our forgiveness, especially if they hurt us in ways that are indescribable. I was in a grief group once with someone whose brother was murdered. I could not imagine how she could forgive the person that murdered her brother. There are some people we truly deem unforgiveable. However, forgiveness is for you, not them. When you withhold forgiveness from someone else, you end up hurting yourself.

I suffer with un-forgiveness at times especially if the person did not express remorse for how they hurt me. I can replay what they said or did over and over in my mind. The interesting thing is that sometimes I feel that some people do not deserve my forgiveness, yet I beg God to forgive me for my mistakes. How hypocritical is that? We cannot embrace forgiveness from God and withhold forgiveness from others at the same time. Forgiveness is a huge part of the process and journey to healing. Forgiveness is a process within itself - it requires you to let go of that pain in order to gain peace and strength from the experience.

You also need to forgive yourself. If you are harboring any personal guilt or shame, it is important to forgive yourself so that you can move on. Do not be bound by guilt.

I struggle in this area especially when it comes to my parenting. I constantly feel like I fail my kids. I make mistakes all the time while being a mom, a single mom at that. Sometimes I do not give my kids enough attention because I am cleaning or working. Sometimes I am moody because of a rough day at work, and feel bad not being as present with my boys as I would like. Sometimes, I think I am a failure as a mom. In those moments, I ask God for forgiveness in my shortcomings and ask Him to help me forgive myself.

Finally, you need to seek out forgiveness when you are the one who was wrong. It is not easy but it is so necessary. I apologize to my sons often when I make a mistake. I always try to seek out forgiveness when I have done something wrong, even when it is not easy. The most important forgiveness we can receive is the forgiveness of our sins through Jesus Christ. When you give your life to Him, you are forgiven and free. Words cannot describe that feeling. You must forgive and be forgiven to heal completely.

Phase #6: Dismantling Fear

Another part of the process is addressing and dismantling fear. After a tragedy occurs, fear has the ability to set in. When Steve died, I had so many fears. How would we survive? Would I be able to take care of my boys alone? Who would teach them to be men? I was so afraid that the boys would be lacking something that I was not able to fill.

I was right about one part, what they lacked I could not fill. I could not replace their father and I cannot teach them how to become men. That was a job for God; I had to rest in the fact that He would fill the void that I could not. My children are His children first; God still had my children's best interest at heart even with all that happened before and after the loss. There was no need to fear! As a mother raising two black boys, one of whom had a disability, I had fear. How can I teach them so that they can survive in today's society? I feared them having the wrong encounter with the wrong person. I feared my younger son not knowing how to "properly" respond to a stranger and it being misinterpreted.

I am realizing more and more each day that I do not need to worry to be afraid for my sons; I need to intentionally pray and expect their protection from God. God has his hands on them. I had to get to the root of my fear concerning my boys. I felt like I was a hypocrite. How can I say I trust God and yet I have fear? I realized that I was not fully trusting God. Why? Because the last time I trusted God fully, He let my husband die. I was afraid to trust God fully because of what He might let happen in the future.

I learned that when we make decisions out of fear, we set ourselves up for self destruction. God does not give us the spirit of fear; we cannot have faith in Him and fear in our hearts. So, we have to make a decision. Are we going to live in faith or fear? My decision is faith. God has been too good to me for me to be living in fear. Sometimes, I write down what God has done for me and the dates. I keep these as a reminder when I am going through a storm. God has already done so much for us and He is just getting started. He can't move where fear lies.

Someone might wonder how to get rid of fear. First, you need to unveil what you are afraid of. Is the fear inside of you real? You would be surprised at how many times the things we fear are not as real as we think. Is this fear from a deep rooted pain, or is this fear passed down from someone else's experience? Take time and ask God to reveal the root of your fear. This process may draw up some past painful experiences and old feelings; complete this process. It may be tiresome and difficult, but you will be better off in the long run. The sooner you begin the work to release yourself from fear, the better.

Next, begin speaking God's Word to that fear. Whatever we feed grows. If you feed your fear, it will grow. If you feed your faith, it will grow. Start declaring verses from the Bible against fear, and command your deliverance from it. These steps may sound very "spiritual" in writing, but in reality, it is a huge challenge. You have to continuously remind yourself of what your end goal is: healing. Even when it seems like you are lying to yourself because you do not have faith to believe God's Word, declare it anyway. You have to speak in faith, even when your mind, will and emotions want to stay in fear.

I remember back when my oldest son Quincy was a few months old, it was a tough time. I was 20 years old with an infant. His father and I had recently split and I was battling severe postpartum depression. Depression has always been a part of my life, but that was definitely my lowest point. One night in March 2007, I swallowed almost half a bottle of pills. I was tired. So tired. I had been hiding my depression for years. Pretending to be okay when I wasn't. Smiling when I felt like crying. Now I was a mother.

Remember, I didn't live with my mother growing up, so I had no clue what I was doing. On top of that, Quincy's father and I were young and trying to figure out so much at a young age. I do not have many regrets in my life (I view them as lessons) but if I were to have a regret, it would be this season. I was mean and bitter –downright nasty at times. I made a ton of mistakes and I even surprised myself with some of the things I said, thought and did. I was trying to be a good mom, get over the breakup, find my way, and I was battling internally with God…all while severely depressed. When I took those pills, I was ready to go. In my eyes, the world would be better off without me; my son would be better off without me.

Thank God, He had other plans. My father took me to the hospital and I stayed for almost two days being evaluated in their psychiatric unit. I attended therapy sessions and had alone time as well. I was with people who had various mental health difficulties. It was an amazing experience, but also very scary. I was afraid I would be viewed as crazy (I had a lot to learn about mental health then). I was afraid that I would fail as a parent. I was afraid to die, but more afraid to live. The process to healing began in that hospital. God began to change my heart then. After leaving the hospital, the process wasn't over. I began therapy and have been in therapy off and on ever since. I re-dedicated my life to God several months after that and started healing spiritually. I wish I could tell you that I am totally healed but I would be lying. I am still healing; still learning and growing. The difference now is I am aware that I need healing, and I am unashamed of that fact. I am willing to seek healing. I also now know where my healing comes from: it comes from God. In the past, I tried to heal myself almost took my life. Now, I seek my healing from God now to regain my peace.

The process to healing, particularly after a tragedy is grueling. It is not a walk in the part but the moment you feel that breakthrough, there is nothing like it! There is nothing like that burst of freedom when God delivers you from something! The moment it doesn't hurt quite like it did before is restoring. The moment you realize that you no longer think about it every second of the day is freeing. The moment God removes the sting from your pain is simply amazing; it speaks to exactly who God is.

The work of going through the process has a purpose too. You gain your strength in the storm. You gain your grit in the storm. You gain your praying power in the storm. I would have never been able to endure 2012 if I did not go through 2007. The healing positioned me to withstand all that God has for me, good and bad. I can now look back on things that devastated me then and see it with fresh perspective now. Things that would have killed me before, barely phase me now. The process hard, but worth it in the end.

I think back to the first few months after Steve died. I had to adjust to doing everything. Steve was the cook in our home; I could barely boil water. I had to learn how to cook to feed my family. I remember googling recipes and bombing them. I remember the looks on my kid's faces when they tried something that I worked hard making. I remember the tears and feelings of being a failure yet again; I cried often but I never gave up. I kept persevering and eventually became a decent cook.

One part of the process is realizing that you have to go at your pace. This is not the time to compare yourself to someone else. Take this journey one day at a time, one moment at a time. When it came to cooking, I started by simply focusing on the next meal. I would make the necessary adjustments, try something different, use a new seasoning and watch it more carefully. I kept telling myself the next meal would be better.

Similarly, in your journey through the healing process, you have to start by telling yourself that tomorrow will be better. You will make the adjustments needed to aid in your healing, so that tomorrow will be better. Notice I never say it will be perfect, just that it will be better. We have to let go of the life we thought we would have or the life we wanted and embrace the life God has for us.

This does not mean that the life God has for us is not as good as the life we wanted. God is able to do more than we could ask or imagine (Ephesians 3:20). The life He has for us is the best life for us.

Sometimes it is hard to see better coming, when you have lost so much. I cannot imagine a love better than the love Steve and I had, but I am believing God for just that. I never thought I could be happy in any way after Steve, but I am happy. I never thought I could accept my life; all parts of it, but I have. The pain will take you places you never imagined you would go, but the process makes you who God has called you to be. I would not be Whitney without those experiences. If I could change it all, I wouldn't. I am finally at peace with the will of God.

The process is not all bad; there are many blessings that occur during the process. Each day you get a little stronger. It may not seem like much or you may not even feel that way in the moment, but it is indeed happening. God is making you stronger each day. You will look back and eventually see how God was with you every step of the way. You will notice that in the midst of tough times God still surrounds you with joy. In the almost five years since Steve passed away, I have had many rough days, but I have had even more awesome days. God has blessed me beyond words over the past few years. There have been open doors, healing, restoration, fun, new beginnings and hope. The pain positioned me to meet some of the most amazing people. Miracles have happened during the process. The process has shown me that I am not just Steve's widow but that I am also God's daughter.

The process can sometimes feel like a battle, but always remember the fight is fixed! God has already won the battle. You must pay your dues during the process. Get serious about getting better and being better for God. Get serious about your healing. This is not the time to be timid and shy. This is the time to fight for your peace and your deliverance. Fight knowing the battle has already been won; the fight is just a part of the process. Fight but fight right, with the armor of God, as described in Ephesians 6.

10 A final word: Be strong in the Lord and in his mighty power. 11 Put on all of God's armor so that you will be able to stand firm against all strategies of the devil. 12 For we[a] are not fighting against flesh-and-blood enemies, but against evil rulers and authorities of the unseen world, against mighty powers in this dark world, and against evil spirits in the heavenly places.

The full armor of God will change your mindset, heart and actions. You must anticipate the enemy to do what he does (steal, kill, and destroy) and also anticipate God to do what He does (restore, renew, heal). Always remember that the weapons will form, they just won't prosper. What does the full armor of God look like?

Let's jump right back into His word picking back up in Ephesians 6:13.

, "13 Therefore, put on every piece of God's armor so you will be able to resist the enemy in the time of evil. Then after the battle you will still be standing firm. 14 Stand your ground, putting on the belt of truth and the body armor of God's righteousness. 15 For shoes, put on the peace that comes from the Good News so that you will be fully prepared.[b] 16 In addition to all of these, hold up the shield of faith to stop the fiery arrows of the devil.[c] 17 Put on salvation as your helmet, and take the sword of the Spirit, which is the word of God."

Each layer is essential for the process. The belt of truth is vital! The truth is in the Word of God. Any thought you have, trace it to the word of God. If it is not there, it is not true. The body armor of righteousness is taking our walk with God to a new level. You are designed by the Most High God, uniquely crafted according to His will. Act like royalty because that is what you are! You do not have to stoop to the enemy's level, let him remain there alone. Carry yourself in a way that pleases God. For the shoes, the Word says put on the peace that comes from God; walk in peace. Walk throughout this process in total peace knowing that God is indeed in control.

The shield of faith will keep you from losing your mind. If God can allow the unimaginable, He can use it to transform your life. Have faith that God will carry you through the hard times, and be prepared to testify when He delivers.

Last but not least, put on the helmet of salvation. God gave us His best, Jesus. Eternal life and forgiveness is available to you because of the cross. There is no sin committed that isn't under the insurance of the cross. With salvation, you are fully covered and the debt has been paid. During this process, remind yourself to whom you belong. The God we serve gave His only son for us; His love runs deep. Jesus loves us so much that He took the greatest pain from us; the cross. If Jesus can carry the cross, carrying your pain is no problem.

Change and Transition

One of most difficult things that occurs during the process is dealing with change and transition. Many times, God will shake up your surroundings during the process towards your healing. After my husband died, I bought a new house, joined a new church and my children started new schools. There was a lot of transition during that time. I met some new friends and lost some friendships as well. All the change and transition during one season can be very hard. It can be overwhelming for many reasons. Take courage in knowing that God strategically orchestrates things for us. Nothing just happens, it is all a part of His plan. It also leads us closer to Him. Sometimes He removes people or things to redirect our focus. I realized there were some friendships I had that I depended on more than I depended on God. I would get their opinion on things before I prayed. I would follow their advice ahead of God's. I looked to them for comfort, not God. Needless to say, when those friendships changed it devastated me. I remember feeling like what did I do wrong? What is wrong with me? Lord, why so much loss?

I realize now that the reason God changed the nature of those friendships was so I could redirect my attention to Him. Those friendships were wonderful but not like my relationship with God. I would go to my friends before I went to God. I would be dependent on them for my healing and not God. God is the ultimate source! When you put your faith in people or things you are bound to come up short. Also, the weight that I carry is meant for a savior! God had to remove some people and positions in order for me to realize that He is my source. Now I can have meaningful friendships but with appropriate boundaries. My hope is not in my friendships. My hope is in Christ.

When you are going through the process, it is important to pray against the victim spirit. I struggled heavily with this. I always felt like the victim. I used to think if people felt sorry for me that would make them love me and not abandon me. Being the victim is draining for you and for those around you. No one wants to be around someone always seeking sympathy or not taking accountability for their actions. No one wants to be around someone always making excuses. It is draining! I can see why people chose to leave my life when I was in this frame of mind. I am so thankful for healing from this mentality.

Once you realize who you are in God, you do not have to try to manipulate people into loving you. You are no longer a slave to people pleasing and seeking approval from others. Yes, the loss and purging of the process can be hard, but the new life introduced is even more amazing. God has restored some old relationships in my life, and sparked some new ones. God gives you just what you need for every season! I have met some awesome people and connected in many ways. I was even blessed to meet some young widows as well. Although I am sad that there are more women dealing with the pain of widowhood, I am so blessed for the community of women He gave me to embark on this journey with. God never takes from you, He just reassigns! I have not arrived – I still have flaws; however, I can truly say that going through this process has brought me so much peace. I give God all the glory for that.

When you are in the process phase, you cannot hide behind the façade that everything is perfect. I was so good at pretending that I could fool myself at times. I could spend the whole day smiling and encouraging others and cry all night. I could pray wholeheartedly for others and not have the energy to pray for myself. I could give a scripture to someone and believe for miracles in their life, but have no faith for myself. I was also believing God for the miracles of others but not believing for myself.

Do not miss out on your healing because you are not committed to doing the work. If you need counseling, or even medication, do not be ashamed. God orchestrates the healing that takes place through counseling and medication just as He orchestrates supernatural healing. All healing comes from Him. Do not get caught up in how your healing looks, get caught up in being healed.

Consistency is key when you are in process. My healing requires continuous counseling, asking for help and taking breaks. My healing requires Jesus. Be consistent with whatever you need to maintain your healing; don't stop after the first time you feel better. Just as pain will return and intensify after only one dose of medicine, such is healing. If you start the process to healing but do not continue, your healing will be temporary.

Although the process looks and feels different for everyone, it is necessary. The process can be grueling, but the purpose is amazing. Don't give up. The process won't kill you, it will mold you. It is the process that reveals your purpose.

Purpose

_I have brought you glory on earth by finishing the
work you gave me to do.
John 17_

After the pain and the process, you might feel overwhelmed and exhausted, but don't be discouraged, we have finally come to the best part - purpose. Did you really think you went through ALL of that for nothing? Of course not! The painful and difficult circumstances that God allows in your life are opportunities for you to help others heal; purpose completes the process. Part of my purpose is writing this book.

This book is not about being a young widow, single mom, mother of a child with autism, etc. This book is about what to do when God's will hurts. Prior to the last few years, I wasn't honest in my relationship with God. I was really hurt by some things that happened in my life but I wouldn't confess that to God. The past few years taught me that if I want a real authentic relationship with God, I was going to have to be real with Him.

Whatever God allowed you to go through serves a purpose.

Galatians 6 gives us some insight into this. " 9 So let's not get tired of doing what is good. At just the right time we will reap a harvest of blessing if we don't give up. 10 Therefore, whenever we have the opportunity, we should do good to everyone— especially to those in the family of faith."

What does this mean? God wants us to take the pain and experiences that He has allowed and use them to bless others.

Purpose is such a fulfilling place to be in once you reach it. It is the moment you realize that your tears were not in vain. It is the moment you see your pain in someone else and you can rejoice because you have been there and can minister encouragement to them. It is the hope in someone's eyes as you share your journey. Pain can sometimes make you feel like you are all alone. That is a trick of the enemy to isolate you. Once you are by yourself, the enemy has you just where he wants you. When you boldly tell your story, you are positioning others to receive their freedom in Christ. Purpose helps you to bless someone else.

How God uses your unique experiences is already determined and was determined before you were even created. God has a unique plan for each of us; He knows exactly what we need to go through in order to fulfill the purpose He has for us. That is the beauty of God, nothing is by coincidence; everything is strategically aligned.

Because of what God has allowed me to experience, I developed a passion for children with disabilities. I developed a special passion for children with autism and emotional disabilities. Even before my son Kevin was diagnosed, I loved these kids and they were drawn to me. The year before Kevin received his diagnosis, I began spending time with an awesome young man with autism, which opened the door for me to receive a job at a non-profit supporting kids with this illness. God was preparing me even though I did not realize it. Rest assured, there is purpose in your pain.

Purpose is not about you; it is about God. It is about telling someone else what God did for you and assuring them that He can help them too. This reminds of testimony service that some churches still do. I love hearing other people's testimonies. It encourages me to keep trusting God. At the appointed time, God will move mightily for me also. God will reveal to you how He wants to use you when you fully submit to Him.

Maybe He wants you to start a non-profit, write a book, lead a ministry, write a song, or develop a business. He may want you to go out and speak publically about your experience. The key to purpose is transparency. This is not the time to be holier than thou. This is not the time to pretend like everything was perfect. This is the time to get real! It is the time to really share how God blessed you but to also explain the process. Sometimes people tell me that I am strong. They compliment me on all that God has accomplished through me. The truth is, it is not about me. God is my strength. I am nothing without Him! I am quick to tell people, "it is all God." I am quick to share that this is not easy. I don't ever want to give the impression that it is all perfect over here; it is not. Being transparent will draw others to Christ. Not everyone was raised in the church and even if they were, everyone's relationship with God is different. Some people are really hurting and a fake testimony is not going to sway them. They need the real. They need the raw truth. They need you operating in your purpose.

Not sure what your purpose is? Look at the things you do daily. Look at the things that you feel you cannot live without. I love kids. I could not imagine not being around kids. I love helping people and making them feel better. These things may lead you to your purpose. Of course there are plenty of spiritual gift tests you could take, but make sure you spend time seeking God in this area. This is the perfect time to go on a fast to hear from God. When God reveals your purpose, do not be afraid. God will equip for all that he needed you to do. I was so nervous to write a book although writing has been a lifelong love of mine. Once I finally submitted to God, writing the book was an amazing experience.

The funny thing about purpose is that the enemy will try to use that against us! He will try to tell us that our purpose is not as significant as someone else's or he will try to make us dislike the purpose God gave us. I have family members and friends who can sing, I mean really sing. They have beautiful voices that will stop you in your tracks. I love music and I love to sing, to myself! I can carry a note, but I am not a singer; that is not my purpose. However, the fact that I am not a singer does not make me less significant than someone else.

God has a lane designated for you; own it! Don't get caught up on what someone else is doing or what you cannot do, get busy doing what God called you to do!

1 Corinthians 12:18-21 says, *"[18] But our bodies have many parts, and God has put each part just where he wants it. [19] How strange a body would be if it had only one part! [20] Yes, there are many parts, but only one body. [21] The eye can never say to the hand, "I don't need you." The head can't say to the feet, "I don't need you."*

We are all needed in the body of Christ. We each bring something unique that is needed and valuable. When we focus on what God needs us to do instead of what He is doing through someone else, we will have more peace! There is enough room in the kingdom of God for us all! There is no need for competition. Just be yourself, it is what God intended.

The moment God reveals your purpose for His kingdom is the moment the enemy takes position. His goal is to keep you away from your purpose. He will do all kinds of things to distract you and get you off track. This is why fasting and praying is essential during this season. You also need community as well. This is the time to a have a few trusted people that you can share your purpose with. This is not to be shared with everyone. Ask God for wisdom and discernment on who to share with. I am an open book and will usually tell anyone anything, but the past few years has taught me discernment. I take time to seek God on what to share and with whom. Not everyone can handle your purpose.

The enemy will use people to block you from your purpose. God knows the people who will cover you in prayer and hold you accountable as you work in your purpose. Seek guidance on who those people are. Also seek guidance on when God wants you to move toward your purpose and what that looks like. God can give you a vision that is not meant to happen for another year. He may give you the vision ahead of time so you can begin to prepare for it physically, mentally, emotionally, spiritually or financially. God does everything in perfect timing (read Ecclesiastes 3) and if you move before it is time, the vision will be off. I like to hit the ground running when I hear from God, but sometimes, He me to be still. God gave me the vision and title for this book in February 2013. I started writing right away. For some reason, it was not working. I couldn't figure out why. It was because it was not time to write. There are things I have experienced in the four years since God gave me the vision that needed to occur in order for me to obtain the growth necessary to write. There was some sin I had to deal with before getting to my purpose.

Sometimes we get so excited and we take on what God said and even more. Before we know it, we are overwhelmed with life. I would rather do a few things in excellence than a million things in mediocrity. Your purpose should not overwhelm you, but excite you. Your purpose should not feel like a burden, but it should be a pull from your heart.

It is easy to get excited and started doing without consulting God. So many times, I have jumped before God said go. God's moves are strategic, not impulsively thrown together without thought. One must take time to seek God for guidance. That is the hardest thing for me, and it requires much prayer. You need to pray and have others praying for you during this time. What I can tell you is when it is time, God will open doors you didn't even know existed! He will move mountains on your behalf!

So, what exactly is your purpose? It is simple: to use your healing to aid someone else in theirs. God uses people to build His kingdom and reach His people. There is one thing we must remember: our purpose is not bigger than God. We can get so excited about the purpose that it is tempting to make that more important than God. This book is a part of my purpose, but this book is not bigger than God. Just like my pain is not bigger than God, my purpose is not either. In all things, we must keep perspective. There is nothing and no one higher than God. Do not allow the pain, the promise, the process or the purpose become your God. God is the only God! You are not defined by what happened to you, you are defined by God.

Make sure that when you walk in your purpose you remain clothed in truth. Sometimes we tweak our story to make it better. We may give ourselves or others credit for what God did. I have a tremendous amount of support and if it weren't for my family, friends, church family and co-workers I do not know where I'd be. However, those people were willing vessels used by God to bless my family. I have accomplished many things but I am not above God! I am a willing vessel used by Him. Nothing that I do for God is bigger than God.

Your purpose can be intimidating. You may even feel afraid of what God is asking you to do. The blessing is God never makes you enter your purpose alone, He is right there with you. There is never a time that God has given an assignment to someone without giving them the tools and support to carry out that assignment. God sends us people to walk along side our purpose. Ask God to send you a mentor and a mentee. This is for you to grow and be held accountable but also for you to lift someone else up as well. There is one key element in turning you pain to purpose: hearing and obeying the voice of God.

Your purpose is amazing and someone's life is dependent on it. In order to reach your purpose, you must be able to hear and discern the voice of God. Many may wonder how to do this. The best ways to learn to hear God's voice is to pray, read His Word and listen to what He says.

You must spend time in prayer to discern how God wants to use you. You must create daily time to spend praying. Prayer is communication with God, it is talking to Him. Prayer is not just about you asking God for things. It is time to repent of your sins and ask for clarity and direction. Ask Him to reveal any struggles that you are facing and to give thanks for what He has done.

Prayer is also a time to listen. You cannot do all the talking in prayer; take time to hear what God has to say. Quiet yourself and pray for an open heart and obedient spirit to hear and obey what God says.

Always remember that everything that God says can be backed up to His Word. This will keep you from confusing God from the enemy. The enemy's words will push you away from God and your purpose instead of leading you to it. The enemy's words will please your flesh. God's words will speak to your spirit.

Lastly, you must read His Word! I have mentioned this numerous times throughout the book because it is so important. God speaks to us through His word just as much as He speaks directly to us and through other people or circumstances. You must make daily devotional time to pray, listen and read His word. Once God has revealed your purpose, you must be willing to move. As you read, you will learn to discern between God and the enemy.

Know that the enemy is cunning. He molds his voice to match voices familiar to you. He can even make his voice sound like yours. You could be speaking death over your own situation using the enemy's voice. The enemy may use those people close to you, or even people you look up to, to pull you away from your purpose. While the enemy plots to destroy, he can only dwell where he has an audience. Cast down the voice of the enemy and echo the voice of God.

God will bless you for carrying out the purpose He has for you. Let's look at what is says in James.

James 1:22-25 says, [22] *But don't just listen to God's word. You must do what it says. Otherwise, you are only fooling yourselves. 23 For if you listen to the word and don't obey, it is like glancing at your face in a mirror. 24 You see yourself, walk away, and forget what you look like.* [25] *But if you look carefully into the perfect law that sets you free, and if you do what it says and don't forget what you heard, then God will bless you for doing it."*

Another passage of scripture that addresses reading the word of God can be found in Proverbs.

Proverbs 4:20-22 says, "*My child, pay attention to what I say.*
Listen carefully to my words.21 Don't lose sight of them. Let them penetrate deep into your heart, 22 for they bring life to those who find them, and healing to their whole body."

God speaks to us in many ways but He always has a message for us in His word! You need the word of God in every area of your life.

When the word of God is in you, you can pull it out of you during a rough patch. What you are full of is what you draw from when suffering. If you are full of bitterness, anger and resentment, that is what will come out of you during the hard times. If you are full of positivity, hope, joy and peace then that will come out of you. Store up hope inside of you by spending time in the Word of God. Hearing the Word in church on Sunday is not enough! Two hours of church cannot defeat a 24/7 enemy. You need daily time in the Word!

Miracles can occur when you walk in your purpose. God will bless you when He sees you doing his will. Our purpose may take us to some rugged places before it takes us to royal palaces. One of my favorite women in the Bible is Ruth, and it is not just because she was a widow like me. Ruth was not of doing hard work. God showed her favor as she was working. When Ruth became a widow, her mother-in-law Naomi gave her a way out. She told her to go back to her people. Naomi thought it would be easier to for Ruth to return to what is familiar to Ruth. However, Ruth had other thoughts. Ruth made it clear that she wasn't going back and that she would follow Naomi wherever she went. Ruth could have went back "home" and things could have been okay. Instead, traveled on a road unknown; what a testament to trust God.

Once we have been transformed by God after devastation, we cannot just go back "home." God positioned us for greater. When Ruth went with Naomi, she had to humble herself and glean in the fields. She was working in the fields to provide for her and Naomi when Boaz noticed her. She was in an unfamiliar place, working. Boaz blessed her and made sure her and Naomi had all they needed.

What I love about this (in Ruth 2) is when Ruth asks Boaz why he is showing her favor. He replies that he heard about how she has treated Naomi and he saw her working in the fields. God will bless you when you walk in your purpose; He will notice when you are doing His will; He will position you for favor. You will have to enter some uncharted territory and be willing to get dirty. Don't let the pain keep you from your purpose. Be obedient and allow God to mold your pain into your purpose.

Do not be fooled into thinking that you can please God by attaching yourself to someone else's purpose. I know Steve's purpose was to teach the Bible. When I get to Heaven I cannot say, "Hey God I'm with Steve, I'm His wife!" I will be held accountable for what I did or didn't do on my own. You can still support the purpose of others while operating in your own purpose.

There is no need to compete; each of us are designed to reach different people. I will not be able to reach the same people as you. I will reach the people God intended for me to reach and so will you. I used to spend so much time wondering if I was good enough. Would I be as effective as this other person? I used to compare myself to others - maybe I do not pray as eloquently as them or know as much scripture. None of that matters to God. He just wants a willing vessel. Allow yourself to be used!

When you are operating in your purpose, remain truthful. Be honest about how you reached this level of peace. This is not the time to forget that it was God who brought you through. Some of us come out of the storm and forget who calmed the rage of the storm. Remain humble; your purpose is about about sharing what God did. Walking in your purpose requires a level of transparency that may be hard for some. It requires you to open up. Remember the goal is exposing others to the healing power of God. We can't do this playing it cool. In my opinion, this is the problem with the body of Christ; we tend to back off when things get rough instead of standing tall. Why aren't we being open and honest about the pain, the promise, the process and the purpose? Why don't we share about those dark places? Are we afraid to be seen in that light? Are we afraid to be seen as imperfect?

The longer we put on the facade, the more opportunities we miss for God. Tomorrow is not promised. Do you really want to leave this world with an unfulfilled purpose because you were too cute to be real with someone? Are you that important that you cannot be transparent and even vulnerable with someone? I am never too cute to be real about what God has done in my life. I am not ashamed to talk about my dark places. Remember, in all things there is discernment. Pray and seek God's counsel on when and what to share with whom. When you move according to the will of God and submit to His timeline, you can rest assure your purpose will be blessed.

Purpose takes you into uncharted territory, and the unknown can be very scary. It requires you to be open to change and transition as well. Remember it is only unknown to you, God knows all things. Do not run from your purpose; embrace it! When I was young, I heard the voice of God. I knew He was calling me to serve Him. I was still trying to figure out who I was, but there was one thing I knew – serving Him wasn't the "it" thing to do. I was already being teased for being a "goody". I didn't drink, smoke or party. I was "boring". I tried so hard to fit in, but it just wasn't me.

When I turned 19 and got pregnant a few months later, everything changed. I was about to become a mother. Having my older son Quincy was the best thing that ever happened to me because he brought me back to God. I wanted to be my best self for my son and I knew I needed to seek God. Your purpose is not going anywhere. You can run and "do you" but guess what? It will be right there waiting for you when you get done! The sooner you submit, the better!

Do not be surprised if your purpose brings its own set of challenges. Your purpose also comes with a price; you will have to make some sacrifices. You cannot be on the fence – you must be all in for Christ and all in for your purpose. You may have to let some people, some places and some things go. God may require you to change jobs or even move. You may come to the place where you have a choice - choose wisely.

I moved around a lot as a kid. I went to four different elementary schools and have lived in more homes I can count. In one year, I moved four times. When I became an adult and more importantly a mother, my biggest goal was stability. I wanted my kids to have one home that they remember. I wanted them to go to the same schools. I wanted stability and comfort. The thing with stability is sometimes in our pursuit of it, we become complacent. Complacency and God's purpose do not mix. You cannot be complacent and do the work of God. You have to be available to God and willing to move.

It is almost like the military personnel who is waiting for their orders. You need to be expecting God to give you an assignment and wiling to move on it. This is easier said than done. I remember when God first gave me the vision of speaking about my pain. I was agitated. I was thinking that it was bad enough that God allowed me to endure so much pain but now I have to relive it by sharing it?! It was all too much. Now, I cannot wait to share what God has done for me. I know this is just the beginning; the unknown is still a bit frightening to me, but I am fully submitted! The reason I am fully submitted is because I would rather have one painful day with God than one thousand happy days without Him. If I help just one person like many people helped me, it is worth it.

Finally, purpose provides community, which is something we all need. I belong to a support group for parents of children with autism and it has been a tremendous blessing to me. It is so rewarding to have people with you on your journey; it gives you hope to endure. The best part is no matter where you are on the journey, you are a valuable member to the group and you are needed. Such is the body of Christ. We all have our own story and we are all in different places in our walk with God. Your story (the good, bad and ugly) is vital to God. It is so necessary that God saw fit to create you. The world would not be complete without you!

Ephesians 2:10 tells us that, "*For we are God's handiwork, created in Christ Jesus to do good works, which God prepared in advance for us to do.*"

Take heart in knowing God specifically designed you. You are a diamond in His eyes. Every time you endure pain or hardship God is simply sculpting the diamond, molding it. Embrace the journey. Walk in your purpose and get ready for God to transform your life!

Final Thoughts

You will keep in perfect peace those whose minds are steadfast, because they trust in you.- Isaiah 26:3

I would love to tell you that I have this all figured out. The truth is I don't. I am not an expert. I am not a therapist, psychologist, or doctor. I am simply a woman who poured her heart out over these pages with the hope that after reading this just one person would choose to trust God another day. This life is not perfect but God has a perfect plan. If you got nothing else from this please just remember this one line:

The pain is REAL, but the promises are ETERNAL!

Your pain is not invalid; it is real. You may truly be hurting and wondering why God allowed you to experience certain things in your life. Please know that God's intention was not to hurt you. God's will is not always pretty, but it is always purposeful. Trust Him and your days will be greater.

You may have turned your back on God. You may have decided to not follow Him anymore. Allow His love to soften your heart. He is standing there waiting for you with open arms. It does not matter what you said, thought or did, He still loves you. Nothing can separate us from the love of God.

Romans 8 describes it beautifully in verses 38 & 39: *For I am convinced that neither death nor life, neither angels nor demons,[k] neither the present nor the future, nor any powers, 39neither height nor depth, nor anything else in all creation, will be able to separate us from the love of God that is in Christ Jesus our Lord.*

If you have left Him, I invite you to come back. If you do not know Him, I invite you to a personal relationship with God. It is not too late; everything you need is in a relationship with him. No matter what you go through, Jesus promises healing, restoration and peace.

If you want to receive salvation, say this prayer and believe it in your heart: *Lord, I am a sinner. I have done great things but also bad things. I have experienced love and pain. Lord, I need you. Come into my life. I confess my sins. I believe that Jesus is the son of God who died for my sins. Lord I cannot keep living like this. Everything I have done is not working.*

Something is missing, it is you. I need you Lord. Please help. In Jesus name Amen.

If you once followed God but disconnected and want to reconnect, please pray this prayer and believe it in your heart: *Lord, I am sorry. Forgive me of my sins. The truth is Lord, the pain broke me. I don't understand how you could allow so much pain. Lord, I am really hurting. I have been trying to handle this on my own and I am tired. Lord, I need you. Help me to make my way back to you. Thank you for your forgiveness. Thank you for your love. It won't be easy but help me get back to that place where you were the head of my life. I need you Lord, please help.*

Wherever you are, it is okay. God loves you anyway. He sees your tears and hears your cries. He wants to love you through this but He will not make you, you have to come to Him on your own. He is there; go to Him. It is time for your healing to begin.

"I will not die but live, and will proclaim what the LORD has done." Psalm 118:17

About The Author

Whitney Hogans is a woman chasing after the heart of God. She is a mother, daughter, educator, public speaker, author and most importantly, child of God. Whitney's only desire is to live a life pleasing to God and to lead others to God. Whitney holds an Associates of Arts degree in Ethics from Mid America Christian University, a Bachelors of Science degree in Special Education from Liberty University, and a Master of Arts degree in leadership in Teaching from Notre Dame of Maryland University. Whitney is currently a Special Education Teacher and the Owner/Author of *She Heals Publishing.* She resides in Maryland with her sons Quincy & Kevin.

CPSIA information can be obtained
at www.ICGtesting.com
Printed in the USA
LVHW03s2127030918
589017LV00010B/660/P

9 780692 870785